Living things
in my
back yard

Bobbie Kalman

Crabtree Publishing Company
www.crabtreebooks.com

Created by Bobbie Kalman

Dedicated by Candice Campbell
For my little sister Jasmine—This will probably apply more to your front yard, but hey, who's counting?

Author and Editor-in-Chief
Bobbie Kalman

Editors
Reagan Miller
Robin Johnson

Photo research
Crystal Sikkens

Design
Bobbie Kalman
Katherine Kantor
Samantha Crabtree (cover)

Production coordinator
Katherine Kantor

Illustrations
Barbara Bedell: pages 1 (all except bats), 8, 11, 14 (woodpecker and raven), 24 (all except wasp and snake)
Anne Giffard: page 21
Katherine Kantor: page 24 (snake)
Cori Marvin: page 1 (bats)
Jeannette McNaughton-Julich: page 14 (white and brown birds)
Bonna Rouse: page 20
Margaret Amy Salter: page 16 (ants)
Tiffany Wybouw: pages 16 (bees and wasps), 24 (wasp)

Photographs
© BigStockPhoto.com: page 13 (bottom)
© Dreamstime.com: page 5 (bottom left)
© iStockphoto.com: front cover, back cover, pages 12 (top), 15
© ShutterStock.com: pages 1, 3, 4, 5 (top), 6, 7, 8, 9 (chipmunk), 10, 11, 12 (bottom), 13 (top), 14, 16, 17, 18, 19, 20, 21, 22, 23, 24
Other images by Digital Vision and Photodisc

Library and Archives Canada Cataloguing in Publication

Kalman, Bobbie, 1947-
    Living things in my back yard / Bobbie Kalman.

(Introducing living things)
Includes index.
ISBN 978-0-7787-3231-0 (bound).--ISBN 978-0-7787-3255-6 (pbk.)

    1. Urban animals--Juvenile literature. I. Title. II. Series.

QL49.K335 2007   j591.75'6   C2007-904243-0

Library of Congress Cataloging-in-Publication Data

Kalman, Bobbie.
    Living things in my back yard / Bobbie Kalman.
        p. cm. -- (Introducing living things)
    Includes index.
    ISBN-13: 978-0-7787-3231-0 (rlb)
    ISBN-10: 0-7787-3231-2 (rlb)
    ISBN-13: 978-0-7787-3255-6 (pb)
    ISBN-10: 0-7787-3255-X (pb)
    1. Animals--Juvenile literature. I. Title. II. Series.

QL49.K2947 2007
591.75'6--dc22
                                            2007027224

Crabtree Publishing Company
www.crabtreebooks.com   1-800-387-7650

Published in Canada
Crabtree Publishing
616 Welland Ave.
St. Catharines, Ontario
L2M 5V6

Published in the United States
Crabtree Publishing
PMB16A
350 Fifth Ave., Suite 3308
New York, NY 10118

Published in the United Kingdom
Crabtree Publishing
White Cross Mills
High Town, Lancaster
LA1 4XS

Published in Australia
Crabtree Publishing
386 Mt. Alexander Rd.
Ascot Vale (Melbourne)
VIC 3032

Contents

Back yards

Do you have a back yard? A back yard is full of **living things**. Plants are living things. Animals are living things. You are a living thing, too!

If you do not have a back yard, visit a park near your home. Make a list of the living things you saw there. Did you see trees? Were there butterflies? Were there people and dogs?

Living or non-living?

Living things need air. Living things need water. Living things need sunshine. Air, water, and sunshine are **non-living things**. Living things need non-living things.

Rocks and water are non-living things. Why do the raccoons need them?

Living things also need food. Many animals look for food in back yards. There are trees, grasses, fruits, and flowers in back yards. Some backyard animals eat these plant foods. Some animals eat other animals. What is this chipmunk eating?

Squirrels and...

If you have trees in your back yard, you also have squirrels. Squirrels live in the trees. They run up and down the tree trunks looking for nuts and **acorns** to eat. They take food from bird feeders, too. Squirrels are on the move all day long. They sleep at night.

Where did this squirrel find some food?

acorns

8

Chipmunks

Chipmunks are small squirrels with stripes on their fur. They are not fussy eaters. They eat fruits, nuts, bird eggs, worms, and insects. Chipmunks can find these foods in back yards. This chipmunk has found a strawberry.

Raccoons around us

Raccoons can live and find food anywhere! They live in forests and fields. They live in cities and find food to eat there. Raccoons find food in people's back yards, too. These raccoons are hiding on a shed roof.

Smelly skunks

Skunks come into people's back yards and dig up the grass. They eat the bugs and worms they find under the grass. People stay away from skunks. Skunks make a bad-smelling spray inside their bodies. When a skunk stomps its feet and lifts up its tail, stay away! It is ready to spray!

Pets or pests?

Do you have a pet? Many children have pet mice, rats, or rabbits. These animals may live in your back yard, too, but they are not pets. They can cause problems.

Rats and mice can be good pets, but the ones in your yard are not safe to touch.

Mice, rats, squirrels, and chipmunks are animals called **rodents**. Rodents have four sharp front teeth that never stop growing. Two teeth are at the top of the mouth, and two teeth are on the bottom. Rabbits are not rodents, but they can be pests. The rabbit above is eating someone's flower.

Rodents chew on wood and wires so their teeth will not grow too long.

13

Backyard birds

Birds are animals with two legs and two wings. Birds also have beaks. Many kinds of birds live in back yards. Some birds fly away to warmer places when winter comes.

These birds are cardinals. The red bird is a male. The brown bird is a female. Cardinals do not fly away during winter.

Some people hang bird feeders in their back
yards. Bird feeders are filled with nuts and
seeds. Bird feeders help birds get enough
to eat in winter when it is hard to find food.
These birds are eating at a bird feeder.

Insects everywhere

Your back yard is full of insects! Insects are small animals. Some insects have wings, and others do not. Some insects make their homes in back yards. Some wasps build **hives** that hang from trees. Most ants build homes under the ground. Ant homes are called **nests**.

There are many places for insects to find food in back yards. Some insects eat leaves and other plant parts. Bees drink **nectar**. Nectar is a sweet liquid inside flowers. Some insects eat other insects!

This insect is a dragonfly. Dragonflies eat flies and mosquitoes. This dragonfly is eating a fly.

Spiders in yards

Have you ever seen a spider web in your back
yard? Many kinds of spiders spin silk webs.
A spider's web is clear and sticky. Insects
get caught in the web and cannot escape.
This garden spider has caught an insect in
its web. The spider will eat the insect.

18

Snails

Snails visit back yards, too. Snails have four **tentacles**, or feelers, on their heads. Their eyes are at the ends of two tentacles. Snails smell with the other two tentacles. Snails eat plants. Snails also eat dead bugs and leaves. They help clean back yards when they eat!

tentacles

Frogs and toads

toad

Do you have a pond in your back yard? If you do, frogs probably live there. Frogs start their lives in water. When they are fully grown, frogs can live on land or in water. Toads are like frogs, but toads live mainly on land. Toads and frogs eat insects.

frog

Backyard reptiles

Sometimes garter snakes and turtles visit back yards, too. Garter snakes do not have **venom**, or poison, inside their bodies. They will not hurt you. Have you ever seen a turtle crawling in your grass? Snakes and turtles are animals called **reptiles**.

garter snake

painted turtle

Backyard visitors

People in different places can get some strange backyard visitors! Which of these visitors have you seen in your yard?

By any chance, have you ever seen two chipmunks dance?

If this alligator came your way, what would you say?

Would it be, "See you later, Gator"?

What if a bear had a ride—in your hammock right outside?

If you saw these lady butterflies

with your very own eyes,

would it seem like a dream?

Have a good look.

They are right here

in this book!

Words to know and Index

woodpecker

birds
pages 9, 14-15

chipmunks
pages 7, 9,
13, 22

acorns

food
pages 7, 8,
9, 10, 15, 17

frogs
page 20

butterfly

wasp

insects
pages 9,
16-17, 18, 20

raccoons
pages 6, 10

rat

rodents
page 13

skunks
page 11

snakes
page 21

spiders
page 18

squirrels
pages 8, 13

Other index words

24

Printed in the U.S.A.